Getting Chickens

by Becca Heddle
Illustrated by Malu Lenzi

OXFORD

UNIVERSITY PRESS

Have you ever thought about keeping chickens in your garden? They are fun, and you can look forward to fresh eggs every day in the future.

Chickens need other chickens to be happy, so you will need to get at least three. They also need <u>plenty</u> of outdoor space. Before getting chickens, it is worth getting some advice from an expert.

Why do you think chickens need <u>plenty</u> of outdoor space?

I wish we had chickens!

Chickens need a coop to sleep in, and to lay eggs in. They also need a run to wander around in. The coop has to be <u>stable</u> so it won't tip over. In the summer, put the coop in the shade so it won't get too hot.

Show me how to stand so that you are really <u>stable</u>. How might you stand if you were not <u>stable</u>?

The thick planks must be strong.

run

Chickens live outdoors, so you need to keep them safe from animals like foxes.

To keep chickens safe, you will need a good fence and a gate that shuts <u>tight</u>. Then foxes and other animals won't be able to get in and the chickens won't wander out. You must always shut the chickens in their coop at night.

If the gate is shut <u>tight</u>, does that mean there are gaps around it when it is closed, or that there are no gaps around it?

Chickens need plenty of fresh, clean water, so you should put drinkers in the coop and in the run. These must be stable so the water doesn't spill.

Place most of the chickens' food in feeders to keep it dry and clean. You can also scatter some little treats on the ground for them.

The chickens can drink from that pot.

Chickens run in all <u>directions</u> and peck at plants. You will need to fence off any plants that you want to keep, as well as ones that are poisonous to chickens.

Chickens like dust baths too! Dust baths make them feel better if they have itchy skin.

Find a space. Can you walk in one <u>direction</u> and then in another <u>direction</u>?

This chicken is in the dust.

If you get chickens, you should plan ahead. Find a friend to look after them when you're away. Your friend will need to give them food and water, open the coop in the morning and shut it at night, and collect the eggs. Get a book of egg recipes too – there are lots of delicious meals you can make using eggs!

Did you know that chickens are one of the closest living relatives to the Tyrannosaurus rex? Chickens don't have teeth, though – that's why they eat grit. The chickens eat the hard little stones to help them break up their food.

The chickens can dash and run!

Think About the Book

Can you remember what chickens need?